Texas, My State
Native Peoples

The Alabama-Coushatta

By Laura B. Edge

Content Review, With Special Thanks

Carlos Bullock
Alabama-Coushatta
Communications and Media Relations Manager

Bryant J. Celestine
Alabama-Coushatta
Historic Preservation Officer

Alabama-Coushatta Tribe of Texas
Livingston, Texas

Your State • Your Standards • Your Grade Level

Dear Educators, Librarians and Parents . . .

Thank you for choosing this *"Texas, My State"* series book! We have designed this series to support the Texas Department of Education's TEKS Texas Essential Knowledge and Skills standards for curriculum studies AND leveled reading. Each book in the series is a **leveled informational text** and has been **written at grade level** as measured by the Lexile Framework for Reading, the ATOS Readability Formula for Books (Accelerated Reader), and the Fountas & Pinnell Benchmark Assessment System for Guided Reading. Photographs and illustrations, captions, and other design elements provide supportive visual messaging to enhance text comprehension. Glossary and Word Index sections introduce key new words and help young readers develop skills in locating and combining information. Comprehension questions provide teachers and parents with tools for additional learning activities and critical thinking development. We wish you all success in using this *"Texas, My State"* book to meet your student or child's learning needs!

Jill Ward, President

Publisher
State Standards Publishing, LLC
PO Box 68
Athens, GA 30603 USA
1.866.740.3056
www.statestandardspublishing.com

Cataloging-in-Publication Data
Edge, Laura B.
　The Alabama-Coushatta / Laura B. Edge.
　p. cm. -- (Texas, my state. Native peoples)
　Includes index.
　ISBN 978-1-93881-333-7 (lib. bdg.)
　ISBN 978-1-93881-340-5 (pbk.)
　1. Alabama Indians--Juvenile literature. 2. Koasati Indians--Juvenile literature. 3. Indians of North America--Texas--History--Juvenile literature. I. Title.
　976.4--dc23

2015945529

Copyright © 2016 by State Standards Publishing, LLC. All rights reserved. No part of this book may be reproduced, stored, or transmitted in any form or by any means without prior written permission from the publisher. Printed in the United States of America, North Mankato, Minnesota, September 2015, 060215.

About the Author
Laura B. Edge has a bachelor's degree in education from the University of Texas at Austin and has studied abroad with the American Institute of Foreign Study. She has taught reading and writing in elementary schools, middle schools, and a community college. Laura is the author of numerous nonfiction books for young people. She enjoys traveling, dancing, riding horses, and watching football games. Laura lives in Texas with her husband, Gerry.

1 2 3 4 5 – CG – 19 18 17 16 15

Table of Contents

The Creation Story. 5
First People 6
The Early Years 9
The Trail to Texas 10
Tribal Villages 13
Social Order 14
Farming, Hunting, and Trade. 17
Crafts 18
Fun and Games 21
Friend Sam Houston. 22
Two Tribes Join Together. 25
Dark Days 26
The Alabama-Coushatta Today 29
Glossary 30
Index. 31
Think About It & Sound It Out 32

Hi, I'm Bagster! Let's check out the native peoples of Texas.

Buzzard made hills and valleys with his long, powerful wings.

The Creation Story

The Alabama Indians and the Coushatta Indians believe that in the beginning, everything was covered with water. There was no earth. A few small animals floated on a raft. They wanted a new home. Beaver went to see if he could find land beneath the water. He dived over the side of the raft. He was a good swimmer, but he could not touch the bottom. Frog went next. He jumped into the water and swam for the bottom. But Garfish chased after Frog, and he had to return to the raft. Next, Crawfish dived in. He swam and swam and reached the bottom of the water.

Crawfish had a wide tail. He used his tail to scoop mud and formed a tall chimney. The top of the chimney stuck up above the water. It spread out and formed a mass of soft earth. The animals thought Crawfish had done a good job. But the earth was too flat. Buzzard flew over the land. He swung his long, powerful wings down and made valleys. He swung his wings up and made hills and mountains.

First People

Crawfish also dug a huge cave below the earth. Abba Mikko, the Great Chief of Earth and Sky, lived in the cave. He grew lonely. So he took clay and made the men and women who would become the Alabama and the Coushatta Indians. The people lived in the cave for many years. They lived in darkness. One day, Abba Mikko left the cave to work on his other creations. The Indians followed his path toward the cave entrance. A large tree stood at the opening to the cave. The people left the cave. Some went to the right of the tree. Others went to the left. This is how one people became two tribes: the Alabama and the Coushatta.

Outside the cave, sunlight warmed the earth. Plants and flowers grew. Animals of all kinds thrived. The people liked this new world. But they were not completely at ease. So they stayed in the cave during the day. They went outside only at night. One night, a mighty owl hooted and scared the people. Many went back inside the cave and never came out again. That is why the Alabama and the Coushatta are so few in number.

Alabama

The state of Alabama and the Alabama River are both named for the Alabama Indians.

Abba Mikko took clay and made men and women.

Hernando de Soto encountered many Mississippian tribes throughout the Southeast.

The Alabama and the Coushatta were part of the southeastern Mississippian culture.

The Early Years

The Alabama and the Coushatta were once separate Indian nations. They had similar beliefs and understood each other's languages. But each language had its own special words. Ancestors of the Alabama tribe were known as Alibamu. They lived in present-day western Alabama and northern Mississippi. Coushatta ancestors were known as Koasati. They lived in eastern Tennessee on the Tennessee River. Both tribes were part of the southeastern **Mississippian** culture. Their society was ordered around **chiefdoms** based on social class. Mississippians built large mounds for temples and burials.

In 1540, Spanish explorer Hernando de Soto came to America to search for gold. The Coushatta chief welcomed him in peace. He invited de Soto and his soldiers to sleep in a nearby village. Some of the Spanish soldiers stole corn from the Indians. The Indians picked up their clubs. They grabbed their bows and arrows. They prepared for battle. De Soto did not have enough soldiers with him to fight. He scolded his men for the theft and left the village. When they were far away from the Indian warriors, the Spanish captured the Coushatta chief. They placed him in chains and threatened to kill him. The Alabama Indians heard how the Spanish treated their neighbors. Both tribes learned not to trust outsiders.

The Trail to Texas

Spanish explorers brought disease to the Indians, and many died. The Alabama and the Coushatta **migrated** to an area near present-day Montgomery, Alabama, to escape the sickness and other tribes. In the 1700s, English and French settlers arrived in Alabama. War broke out between England and France. France lost the war. So the French had to move west across the Mississippi River. The Coushatta moved west into present-day Louisiana, along with their friends, the French. The Alabama also drifted west. Some settled along the Red River. Others moved toward the Sabine River. By the late 1700s, both tribes had begun moving into Texas. In 1803, the United States bought a large piece of land from France known as the Louisiana Purchase. It included land where the Alabama and the Coushatta lived. Settlers moved in, and the Indians moved farther west. The Alabama settled on the Angelina and Neches Rivers. The Coushatta built villages along the Trinity River.

The Alabama and the Coushatta settled in a region of East Texas called the Big Thicket. This area was rich in **natural resources**. It had prairies, rolling hills, thick woods, and wetlands. The soil was rich and black. Bear, deer, and bison roamed freely. Nearby rivers were full of fish. The Indians liked the area because it was similar to their homelands in Alabama.

Today, the Big Thicket National Preserve is part of the National Park System. It contains one of the most diverse varieties of plant and animal species in the world.

The Big Thicket reminded the Alabama and the Coushatta of their homelands in the Southeast.

The Alabama and the Coushatta migrated from their homelands to the Texas Big Thicket.

The Alabama and the Coushatta lived in log cabins, unlike many other Texas Indians.

Log cabin villages were clustered near rivers.

Tribal Villages

Alabama villages in Texas were clustered in today's Tyler County. Their Coushatta neighbors lived in nearby Polk and San Jacinto counties. Both tribes built their villages near rivers. In the center of the village sat a square. The square was used for religious ceremonies and dancing. The people lived in log cabins. Men cut trees and let them dry in the forest for several months. Then they cut the trees into logs for the walls and poles for the **rafters**. Next, they made shingles for the roof. Men built a chimney at one end of the cabin. They lined the chimney with clay mixed with moss. Each home had enough land around it to grow crops and plant fruit trees. Homes were connected to each other by a series of trails.

Men cleared the land and planted crops. Men also helped the women with household chores. During hunting season, women did all of the housework because the men were out looking for game animals.

The Green Corn Dance was a yearly dance of thanksgiving. Tribal members celebrated good crops. They looked forward to peace and success in the coming year.

Social Order

Clans were the main family unit among the Alabama and Coushatta tribes. Women held important roles in the clan. A child was born into its mother's clan because mothers were seen as the givers of life. The oldest mother in each clan was known as the clan mother.

Each tribe was ruled by a chief and a second chief. Both were elected by the clan mothers. Chiefs were known as **mikkos**. They served lifetime terms. The mikko spoke for the tribe at meetings. He handled disputes between tribal members. He also directed hunts. A man and woman who wished to marry had to ask the mikko for his approval. The mikko chose where to build a home for the couple. He also chose the piece of land where the couple would grow crops. Then the man built the house. When it was finished, he went to the home of his bride and led her to her new home. Once the home was built, women were the owners of the home. Sometimes nephews, brothers, or uncles of the woman lived in the home, too. They moved out when they married. Men and women from the Alabama tribe and the Coushatta tribe often married. But marriage within a clan was not allowed, since members of the same clan were considered relatives.

The oldest mother in each clan was known as the clan mother.

Families sometimes included nephews, brothers, or uncles of the woman who owned the home.

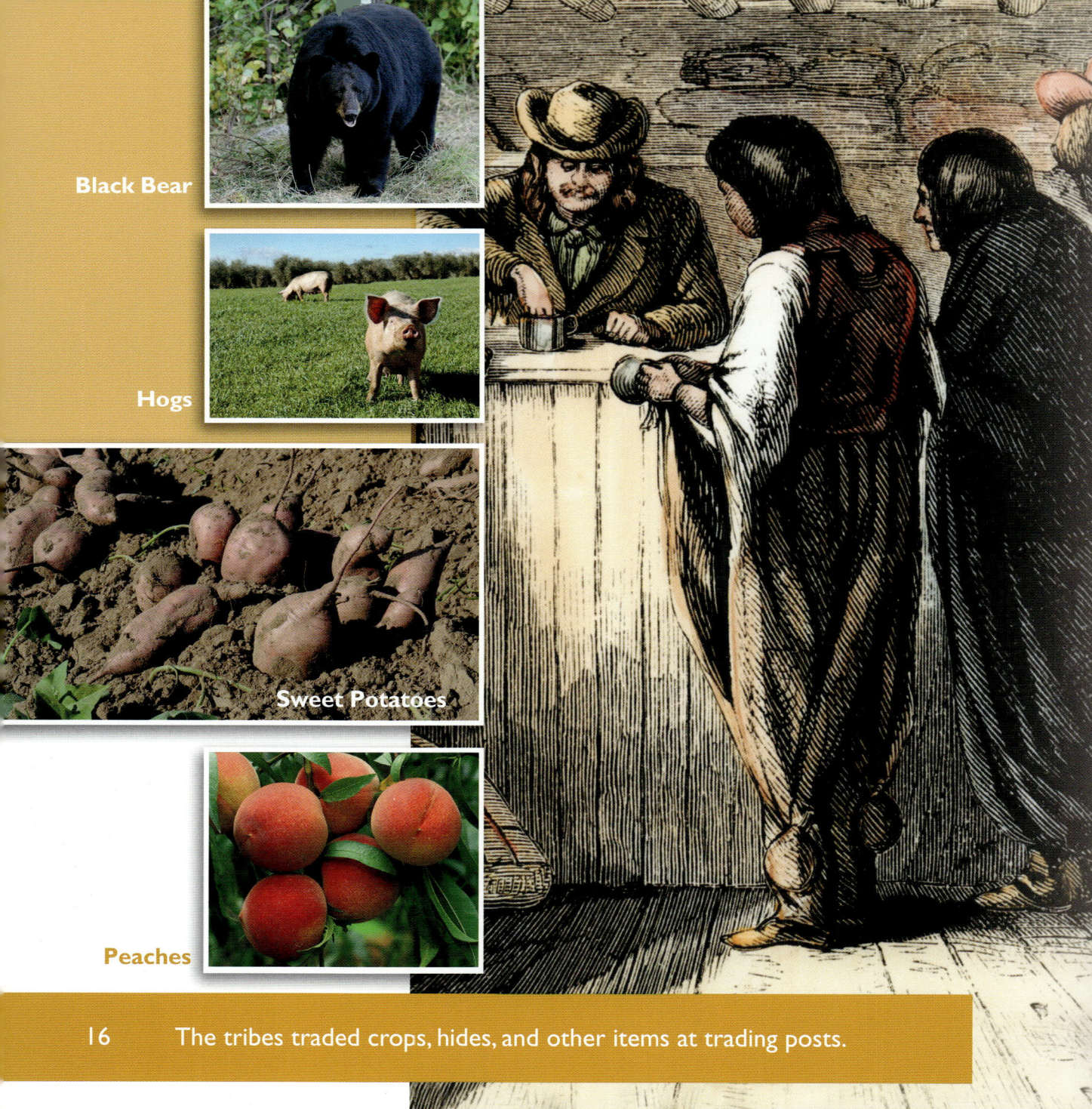

Black Bear

Hogs

Sweet Potatoes

Peaches

16　The tribes traded crops, hides, and other items at trading posts.

Farming, Hunting, and Trade

The Alabama and the Coushatta depended on the land for survival. Villages were based on farming and hunting. Men and women grew corn, sweet potatoes, beans, squash, and other crops. They also planted peach and other fruit orchards. Both tribes raised hogs, cattle, and horses. In the winter months, men hunted bear, bison, and deer. Bear was their favorite meat. On hunting trips, small groups of hunters tracked animals on the prairies. They shot deer and other large game animals with bows and arrows. They killed small animals like birds and rabbits with blow guns made from long lengths of river cane.

Women went with the men on these trips. They cut up and smoked the meat. They scraped and tanned the hides to make clothing, blankets, and moccasins. The tribes traded their extra crops at Spanish or American trading posts. They also traded bear oil and animal hides. In exchange, they received clothing, blankets, wheat, tools, and weapons.

Crafts

Alabama and Coushatta women wove baskets out of river cane stalks. They also used pine needles, sweet grass, or honeysuckle vines. Baskets were beautiful as well as useful. They often had animal designs or were made in the shape of an animal. Women hung baskets on the walls of their cabin to store food and other things.

Women also made pottery out of clay. They dug the clay from the forest floor and left it in the sun to dry. Then they used stones to grind the clay into powder. They added water to the powder and mixed it until all the lumps were gone. When the clay was smooth and soft, the women rolled it until it formed a long tube. They placed one tube or roll on top of another. In this way, they could make bowls and containers of different shapes. They added decorations around the rim of the pottery using their fingers, paddles, stones, and shells. Sometimes they drew shapes and patterns. Other times, they drew animals. They dried the finished container in the sun. Then they placed it in the fire to make the pottery strong.

Pine needle baskets are still woven today.

Pottery was often decorated using fingers, paddles, stones, or shells.

Stickball is still played today by many American Indian tribes.

20 Stickball was used to teach strength and endurance.

Fun and Games

Alabama and Coushatta men played a game called chunkey. They carved a small disc out of wood or stone. To play the game, they tossed the disc onto the ground. Whoever shot an arrow or threw a stick closest to the disc won the game. Men also played stickball. In this game, a ball was tossed in the air. Players made a long stick with a loop on the end to toss the ball. The object of the game was to get the ball through a goal in the middle of the field. It was a rough game, and injuries were common. Men often used stickball games to teach their sons strength and endurance. They also played stickball to settle disputes between tribes. In this way, the tribes could avoid war and many deaths.

Dancing was an important part of Alabama and Coushatta culture. In early times, it was a form of prayer and thanksgiving. There were dances for each animal and crop. There were also victory dances and war dances. The people made music for the dances by putting stones inside turtle shells. They laced the shells together to make a rattle. Drums were used to keep a steady beat.

Rattles were made from turtle shells.

Friend Sam Houston

In 1836, Texans fought to cut their ties to Mexico. Both the Texans and the Mexicans worried about the Alabama and the Coushatta. The tribes lived in the middle of the fighting. If they joined the battle, it could make a huge difference in who won the war. General Sam Houston was the commander of the Texas army. He met with leaders of the tribes. He advised them to stay out of the fighting. They had no reason to risk their lives for either side. Also, when the war was over, no one could be angry with the Indians.

The Alabama and the Coushatta did not fight in the Texas war for independence. When the war ended, leaders of the tribes asked their friend, Sam Houston, for help. The Texas congress set aside a piece of land in East Texas for each tribe. The land would belong to the tribes. No white settlers would be allowed to live there. But settlers ignored the law and continued to move onto Indian land.

As a teenager, Sam Houston lived among the Cherokee Indians in Tennessee. They adopted him into the tribe, and he learned their ways. John Jolly became his Cherokee father. For the rest of his life, Houston had great respect for Indians. He worked hard to make sure they were treated fairly by white people. Houston became the first president of the Republic of Texas.

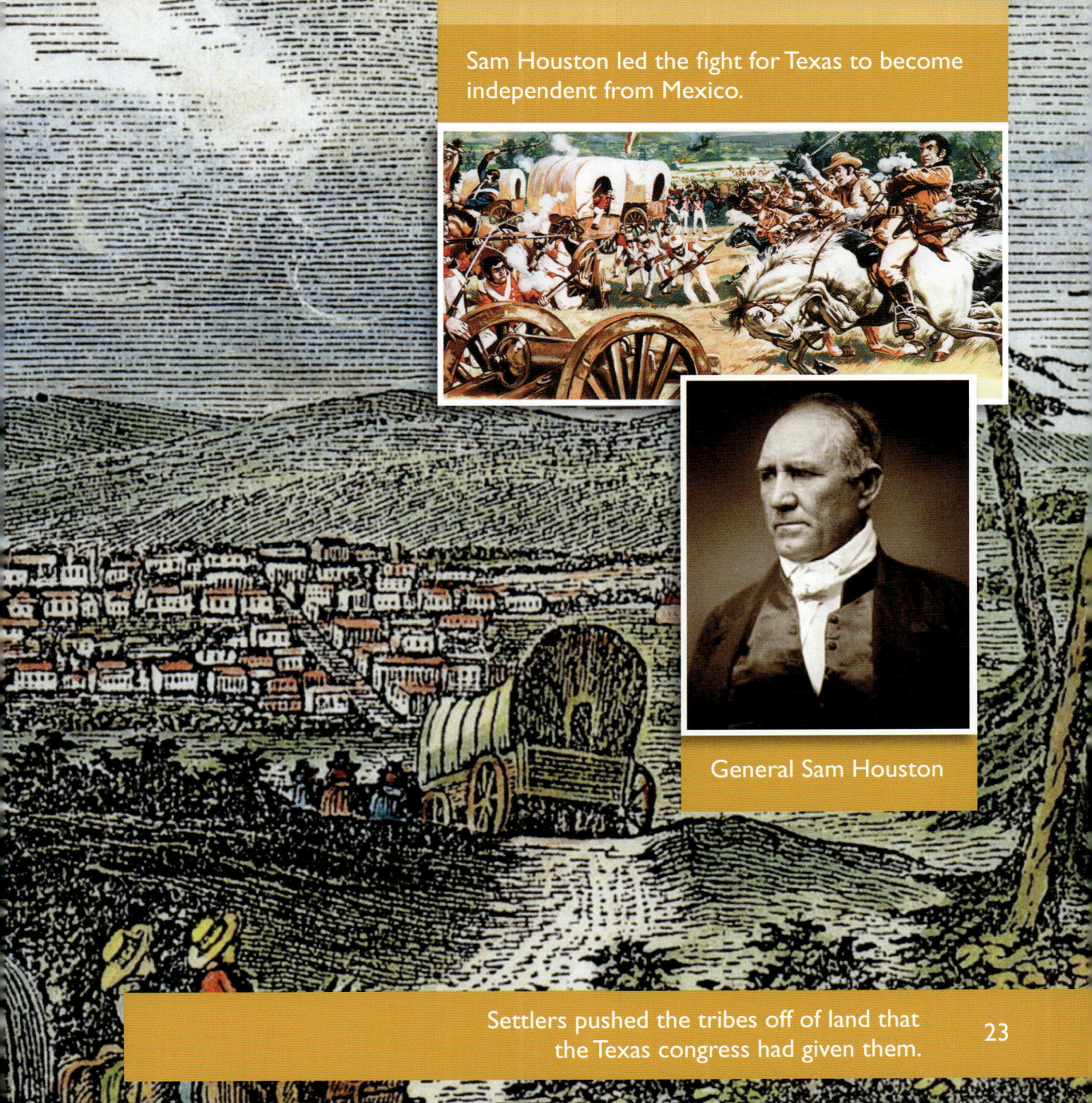

Sam Houston led the fight for Texas to become independent from Mexico.

General Sam Houston

Settlers pushed the tribes off of land that the Texas congress had given them.

The Alabama invited the Coushatta to live on their land.

Two Tribes Join Together

The Alabama and Coushatta tribes both wanted their own land. They did not want to share it with **Anglo** settlers. But settlers kept coming. Before long, there were more settlers than Indians in East Texas. In 1845, Texas became a U.S. state. Leaders of the Alabama tribe asked the state of Texas for land they could keep. In 1854, the Texas congress gave the Alabama tribe 1,110 acres of land near present-day Livingston along Big Sandy Creek. This **reservation** was to be their home. Nobody could take it away from them. Sam Houston advised the Indians to never let a white man live on the reservation. That way, the land would be theirs forever.

One year later, the state of Texas set aside money to give the Coushatta tribe 640 acres of land. But settlers were already living in the area. Some of the settlers let members of the tribe live on their property. Other tribal members roamed the area, looking for a place to call home. The Coushatta asked the Alabama if they could live on their reservation. The Alabama agreed.

The Alabama and the Coushatta were the first tribes to be given a reservation in Texas. The U.S. government forced Indian tribes from the eastern United States to move to Indian Territory. This was land set aside for them in Oklahoma. Many Indians died during the journey. It became known as the Trail of Tears. The Alabama and Coushatta were able to avoid removal because of their peaceful relationship with their Anglo neighbors in East Texas.

Dark Days

As the years went by, life on the reservation grew difficult. Some of the tribes' white neighbors did not want the Indians to become civilized or educated. They cleared the forest to build homes. They stole livestock and burned crop fields in an attempt to drive the Indians away. Game animals became hard to find. The sandy soil on the reservation was poor for farming. Food became scarce, and many Indians went hungry. Some went to work cutting timber in logging camps. Others worked as farm hands for white settlers. The population of the tribe shrank.

Other white settlers saw the poverty of the Alabama and the Coushatta and wanted to help. In 1881, concerned neighbors built a Christian church for the Indians. Teachers, doctors, and ministers worked on the reservation. J. C. Feagin and Clem Fain, two Anglo attorneys in Livingston, wrote letters to the government asking for help for the tribes. In 1918, the U.S. government looked closely at living conditions on the reservation. Their report revealed the needs of the Indians. In 1928, the government loaned money to the two tribes. The state of Texas also tried to help by adding a **grant**. The tribes used the money to build a one-room schoolhouse. They bought livestock and built homes with electricity and indoor plumbing. The tribes also bought land to add to the reservation. The **deed** was issued to the Alabama and the Coushatta Indian Tribes of Texas. After this, the name Alabama-Coushatta Tribe of Texas was used to refer to the united tribe.

The tribe built a one-room schoolhouse with money from the state of Texas.

Many Indians worked as farm hands for white settlers.

Reservation Greetings

Tribal Seal

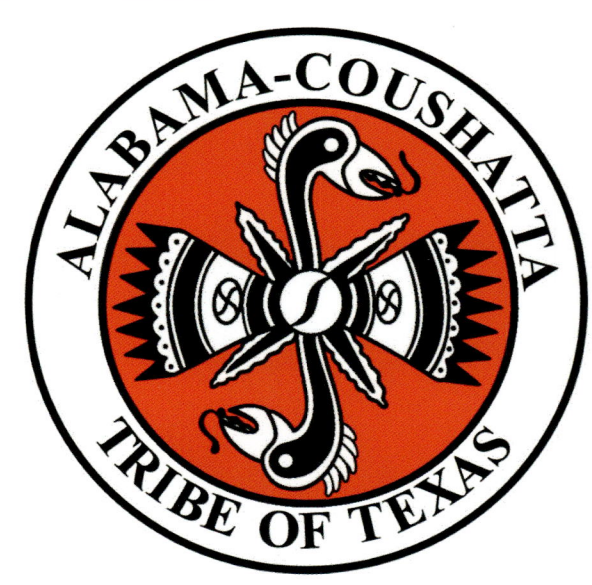

Lake Tombigbee

The Alabama-Coushatta Today

The government continued to help the tribe. They built homes on the reservation. They built a hospital and gave medical aid. They also built a kindergarten to get children ready for public school. Close contact with Anglos changed Alabama-Coushatta culture. Many members of the tribe began to practice the Christian religion. They learned the English language and dressed like their white neighbors. Children played basketball and volleyball instead of chunkey and stickball. But the tribe held on to its traditions. They handed down stories of the old ways from parents to children. They continued to thrive.

Today, the Alabama-Coushatta Tribe of Texas is governed by a seven member tribal council. Its members are elected by the people. The reservation now has almost 5,000 acres with a large lake, called Lake Tombigbee. Tourists picnic, swim, and camp around the lake. Each June, the Alabama-Coushatta Tribe holds a modern **powwow** to celebrate its heritage. Dancers wear **regalia** in remembrance of the dances of the past. The tribe also celebrates and demonstrates modern-day skills.

Many American Indian tribes no longer exist. As a people, the Alabama-Coushatta have adapted and endured. They remind us of our past. And they point to a bright future where different groups of Americans live in peace with each other.

Glossary

Anglo – A white American of non-Hispanic descent.

chiefdom – Independent communities under the rule of an important chief, usually in Mississippian societies.

clan – A type of large family group.

deed – A legal document by which a person transfers ownership of buildings, property, or other items to another person.

grant – Something legally given to another, such as property or money, usually for a project or special purpose.

migrate – To move from one country or region to another.

Mississippian – Mound-building societies of the Southeast made up of multiple chiefdoms and structured around social class.

mikko – A leader or tribal chief.

natural resources – Things that come directly from nature that are useful to humans.

powwow – An American Indian ceremony or social gathering that celebrates traditional and modern-day culture.

rafters – Large beams that support a roof, which are usually made of wood or steel.

regalia – The clothing and ornaments worn by American Indians during powwows or other formal occasions.

reservation – An area of land set aside by the U. S. government for American Indians.

Index

Abba Mikko, 6
Alabama, 9, 10
America, American, 9, 17, 21, 29
Anglo, 25, 26, 29
animal, 5, 6, 10, 13, 17, 18, 21, 26
arrow, 9, 17, 21
basket, 18
battle, 9, 22
bear, 10, 17
Big Thicket, 10
bison, 10, 17
blanket, 17
bow, 9, 17
celebrate, 13, 29
ceremonies, 13
chief, chiefdom, 6, 9, 14
Christian, 26, 29
chunkey, 21, 29
clan, 14
clothing, 17
corn, 9, 17
crop, 13, 14, 17, 21, 26
culture, 9, 21, 29
dancer, dancing, 13, 21, 29
deed, 26
deer, 10, 17
disease, 10
England, English, 10, 29
explorer, 9, 10
family, 14
farming, 17, 26
fish, 10
food, 18, 26
France, French, 10
fruit, 13, 17
government, 25, 26, 29
grant, 26
horse, 17
Houston, Sam, 22, 25
hunt, hunting, 13, 14, 17
Indian, 5, 6, 9, 10, 21, 22, 25, 26
land, 5, 10, 13, 14, 17, 22, 25, 26
language, 9
leader, 22, 25
log cabin, 13, 18
Mexican, Mexico, 22
mikko, 6, 14
Mississippi, 9, 10
Mississippian, 9
moccasins, 17
mound, 9
nation, 9
natural resources, 10
neighbor, 9, 13, 25, 26, 29
plant, planted, 6, 10, 13, 17
pottery, 18
powwow, 29
rafters, 13
regalia, 29
religion, religious, 13, 29
reservation, 25, 26, 29
river, 9, 10, 13, 17, 18
settle, settler, 10, 21, 22, 25, 26
Soto, Hernando de, 9
Spanish, 9, 10, 17
tanned, 17
Tennessee, 9, 22
tool, 17
trading, traded, 17
tribe, 6, 9, 10, 13, 14, 17, 21, 22, 25, 26, 29
United States, 10, 25, 26
village, 9, 10, 13, 17
war, 10, 21, 22
weapon, 17

Editorial and Image Credits

Designer: Jeana Schroeder, Corporate Graphics, North Mankato, Minnesota

Images © copyright contributor unless otherwise specified.

4/5 – "Creation" by Diego Rivera/Bridgeman Images/2015 Banco de México Diego Rivera Frida Kahlo Museums Trust, Mexico, D.F./Artists Rights Society (ARS), New York. **6/7** – "The Creation of Man" by Diego Rivera/Bridgeman Images/2015 Banco de México Diego Rivera Frida Kahlo Museums Trust, Mexico, D.F./Artists Rights Society (ARS), New York. **8/9** – Mississippians: NativeStock; De Soto: "Discovery of the Mississippi" by William Henry Powell. **10/11** – "Indians on the Bayou" by Alfred Boisseau. **12/13** – "Farmstead" by Carlyle Urello, Frank H. McClung Museum, University of Tennessee, Knoxville; Log cabin: Courtesy of Alabama-Coushatta Tribe of Texas; Dance: NativeStock. **14/15** – "Indians by the Fire" by Joseph Henry Sharp/Christie's Images/Bridgeman Images; Elder: NativeStock. **16/17** – Trading post: Northwind Picture Archives; Bear: Diginatur/Wikipedia; Hogs: IHervas/Depositphotos; Peaches: Courtesy Georgia Department of Economic Development; Potatoes: USDA/Flickr. **18/19** – "Carolina Potters" by Martin Pate, pateart.com; Basket: Beverly Moseley/USDA-NRCS/Courtesy of NRCS and the National Agroforestry Center, University of Nebraska-Lincoln/Flickr. **20/21** – Games: Northwind Picture Archives; Sticks: Turtle Track/Wikipedia; Players: Courtesy of Choctaw Nation/Wikipedia. **22/23** – Settlers: Granger Images; "Sam Houston" by C. L. Doughty/Look and Learn, Bridgeman Images; John Jolly: "Col-lee" by George Catlin/Smithsonian Institute of American Art; Sam Houston: Oldag07/Wikipedia. **24/25** – Indians: Northwind Picture Archives; Trail of Tears: Granger Images. **26/27** – Farmer: Lantern Press; Schoolhouse: Courtesy of Alabama-Coushatta Tribe of Texas. **28/29** – All: Courtesy of Alabama-Coushatta Tribe of Texas.

Think About It

Use the information from the book to answer the questions below.

1. What factors caused the Alabama and the Coushatta to move from their original homelands and finally settle in Texas?

2. How did the Alabama and Coushatta tribes' origin in the Southeast affect their culture? What parts of this culture did they bring with them to Texas? How did it make them different from many other Texas tribes?

3. Describe the changes to the Alabama-Coushatta culture that came about after they settled permanently on their reservation in Polk County.

4. White settlement created change for American Indian tribes, like the Alabama-Coushatta. Describe some of the relationships the Alabama and the Coushatta had with their Anglo neighbors. Write your opinions about these. Include both positive and negative experiences.

5. Describe how present-day Alabama-Coushatta people blend their ancient traditions with modern 21st-century culture. How have they adapted? In what ways have they held on to their culture?

Sound It Out

Alibamu: **ah-lee-bah-moo**
Abba Mikko: **ah-bah mee-koh**
Coushatta: **coo-shah-tuh**
Koasati: **koh-uh-sah-tee**
mikko: **mee-koh**